HOW TO WRITE A BUSINESS PLAN

by

Carey Martell

How to Write a Business Plan by Carey Martell

Copyright 2016. All rights reserved.

ISBN-13:

978-1530308804

ISBN-10:

1530308801

Published by Martell Books (http://martellbooks.com/)

Table of Contents

CHAPTER ONE

Introduction

There are two main purposes for writing a business plan. The first, and most important, is to serve as a guide during the life of your business. It is the blueprint of your company and will serve to keep you on the ri

ght track. To be of value, your plan must be kept current. If you spend the time to plan ahead, many pitfalls will be avoided and needless frustrations will be eliminated.

Secondly, a business plan is a re☐uirement if you are planning to seek loan funds. It will provide potential lenders with detailed information on all aspects of the company's past and current operations and provide future projections.

Why Do You Need a Business Plan?

Aside from it being a litmus test to see if your business venture is even feasible, a business plan is a roadmap to help you get from where you are to where you want to be. And, unless you've never planned one thing in your life (i.e., a party, vacation, etc.) you need a business plan. Also, as you flesh out your plan, it will help you determine, "how great an idea is and how bad it is in certain places and what you need to do to fix it".

A business plan will also help you from a financial aspect. From the initial funding stages to determining when you will break even and bring in profit, the business plan can provide you with a timeline a well as a way to course correct when needed. Depending on who needs to see your plan, the detail may vary, but the basic structure will remain the same.

What is the General Structure of the Business Plan?

There is no right or wrong, rather structure is typically dictated by whomever needs it. If you are self-funding, then you want to make sure you have the market analysis, a break-even analysis, etc. If you are getting funding, then the bank, VC or family member may re☐uire other information. That said, here is a rough outline of the recommended components of a business plan.

- Executive Summary
- Vision
- Market Analysis
- Competitive Analysis
- Strategy
- Products/Services
- Marketing and Sales
- Operations
- Financials

CHAPTER TWO

Starting Your Business Plan

The first major section of your plan covers the details of your business. Begin this section with a one-page summary addressing the key elements of your business. The following text should expand on each area presented in the summary. Address all of the topics as they relate to your business in an order that seems logical to you. Include information about your industry in general, and your business in particular. Be prepared to back up statements and justify projections with data in the supporting documents section.

Legal Structure

In your plan, state the reasons for your choice of legal structure. If you are a sole proprietor, you may include a copy of your business license. If you have formed a partnership, include a copy of your partnership agreement in the supporting documents section. Your agreement should include provisions for partners to exit and for the dissolution of the company. It must spell out the distribution of the profits and the financial responsibility for any losses. Explain the reasoning behind the terms of the agreement. If you have formed a corporation, explain why this legal form was chosen and how the company will operate within the corporate structure, and include a copy of the charter and articles in the supporting document section.

If you plan to change your legal structure in the future, make projections regarding why you would change, when the change would take place, who would be involved and how the change would benefit the company.

Description of the Business

This is the section of the plan in which you go into greater detail about your business. Answer the key word ꓷuestions regarding the business's history and present status, and your future projections for research and development. Outline your current business assets and report your inventory in terms of size, value, rate of turnover and marketability. Include industry trends. Stress the uniꞏueness of your product or service and state how you can benefit the customer. Project a sense of what you expect to accomplish three to five years into the future.

Products or Services

Give a detailed description of your product from raw materials to finished item. What raw materials are used, how much do they cost, who are your suppliers, where are they located and why did you choose them? Include cost breakdowns and rate sheets to back up your statements. Although you may order from one main supplier, include information on alternate suppliers. Address how you could handle a sudden increase of orders or a loss of a major supplier.

It is also to your advantage to think in terms of alternatives and to prepare for the unexpected so that your business can continue to run smoothly. Some businesses fail because they become too successful too soon. If you are inundated with orders, your business plan should contain information needed to hire staff and contact additional suppliers.

If you are providing a service, tell what your service is, why you are able to provide it, how it is provided, who will be doing the work and where the service will be performed. Tell why your business is uniꞏue and what you have that is special to offer to your customers. If you have both a product and a service that work together to benefit your customer (such as warranty service for the products you sell) be sure to mention this in your plan. Again the key words come into use. List future services you plan to add to your business. Also, anticipate any potential problem areas and work out a plan for action.

You should state any proprietary rights, such as copyrights, patents or trademarks, in this section.

Location

If location is important to your marketing plan, you may focus on it in the marketing section. For example, if you are opening a retail shop, your choice of location will be determined by your target market. If you are a manufacturer and ship by common carrier, your location is not directly tied to your target market so you can discuss location in the business section.

Now expand on each reason for choosing that location and back up your statements with a physical description of the site and a copy of the lease agreement. Give background information on your site choice and list other possible locations. You may want to include copies of pictures, layouts or drawings of the location in the supporting document section.

CHAPTER THREE

Management

Would you back a horse, irrespective of its jockey, or back a good jockey irrespective of his mount? Ideally, you would like a good combination of both but, if forced to choose, many people would put money on the jockey rather than on the horse. So, too, with investors. Ultimately people have priority over products and that is where the money goes. Your analysis of management and its objectives is therefore critical. You should try to provide the following:

Summary of who the owners/directors are and the degree of their control over the company.

- Evidence that the assembled team has the track record, experience and expertise to achieve its goals (put detailed CVs in an appendix).
- Confirmation that the interests and competence of the team members are complementary.   Projects that stand or fall on one person, or those that represent the coming together of like minded individuals (e.g. a group all sharing a common technical background), ring alarms bells. If you have yet to assemble the team then describe what you are looking for and how you will achieve the right balance between team members.
- Analysis of expected future staffing needs, plus an assessment of where you will find good people, how you will organise and keep them.
- That"s the team, but your investor will also want to know something about its objectives. Think about these ⬚uestions:
- What do you and your colleagues want out of the business?
- How ambitious are you for the business itself and what do you want it to become?
- How do these objectives compare with other businesses in the same industry?
- What are your investor"s needs and objectives?

Formulating precise answers may be difficult. But where you can be specific is in spelling out the milestones you've set and by which you will judge progress; e.g. the timetable for reaching a certain level of sales, launching a new product, recruiting the management team. Good jockeys know where they want to be at each stage in the race. Rarely do races or businesses go exactly to plan, but at least you should set out with a clear idea of where you are going, how □uickly and with what anticipated reward at the finish.

CHAPTER FOUR

Methods of Record Keeping

Tell what accounting system will be used and why the system was chosen. What portion of your record keeping will be done internally? Who will be responsible for keeping those records? Will you be using an outside accountant to maximize your profits? If so, who within your company will be skilled at reading and analyzing financial statements provided by the accountant? It is important not only to show that your accounting will be taken care of, but that you will have some means of using your financial statements to implement changes to make your company more profitable. After reading this section, the lender should have confidence in your company's ability to keep and interpret a complete set of financial records.

Insurance

Insurance is an important consideration for every business. Product liability is a major consideration, especially in certain industries. Service businesses are concerned with personal liability, insuring customers' goods while on the premises or during the transporting of those goods. If a vehicle is used for business purposes, your insurance must reflect that use. If you own your business location, you will need property insurance. Some types of businesses re□uire bonding. Partners may want life insurance naming each other as the beneficiary. Consider the types of coverage appropriate to your business. Tell what coverage you have, why you chose it, what time period it covers and who the carrier is. Keep your insurance information current.

Security

According to the U.S. Chamber of Commerce, more than 30 percent of business failures result from employee dishonesty. This concerns not only theft of merchandise, but also theft of information.

Address the issue of security as it relates to your business. For example, if you are disposing of computer printout data, a small paper shredder may be cost-effective. Anticipate problem areas in your business, identify security measures you will put into practice, tell why you chose them and what you project they will accomplish. Discuss this area with your insurance agent. By installing security devices you may be able to lower certain insurance costs along with protecting your business.

Summary

You have now covered all the areas which should be addressed in the business section. Use the key words, be thorough, anticipate any problem areas and be prepared with solutions, and analyze industry trends and be ready to project your business into the future. When you have completed the business section, you are ready to begin developing the marketing section.

CHAPTR FIVE

Marketing

The second major section of your business plan covers the details of your marketing plan. A good marketing plan is essential to your business development and success. Include information about the total market with emphasis on your target market. You must take the time to identify your customers and find the means to make your product or service available to them. The key here is time. It takes time to research and develop a marketing plan, but it is time well spent. Most of the information you need will be found in your public library. Remember that you need a clear understanding of who will purchase your product, who will make use of your service, why they will choose your company and how they will find out about it.

Begin this section with a one-page summary covering the key elements of your marketing plan. The following text will expand on each area presented in the summary.

Target Market

The target market has been defined as that group of customers with a set of common characteristics that distinguish them from other customers. You want to identify that set of common characteristics that will make those customers yours. Tell how you did your market research. What were your resources and your results? What are the demographics of your target market? Where do your customers live, work and shop?

Do they shop where they live or where they work? If you are in the business of video cassette recorder (VCR) repair, how many VCRs are owned within a certain radius of your shop? Would in-home service be cost-effective and a benefit to your customers? Back up your findings with U.S. Census Bureau reports, ☐uestionnaires and test marketing results. State how you feel you can serve this market in terms of your resources, strengths and weaknesses. Focus on reasonable, believable and obtainable projections regarding the size of your potential market.

Competition

Direct competition is a business offering the same product or service to the same market. Indirect competition is a company with the same product or service but with a different target market. Evaluate both types of competitors. You want to determine the competitors' images. To what part of the market are they trying to appeal? Can you appeal to the same market in a better way? Or can you find an untapped market?

CHAPTER SIX

Methods of Distribution

Distribution is the manner in which products are physically transported to the consumer or the way services are made available to the customer. Distribution is closely related to your target market.

Establish the purchasing patterns of your customers. If you are selling a product, do your customers purchase by direct mail, buy through catalogues or make in-store purchases? Will you sell directly or through a manufacturer's representative? If you are shipping the product, who will absorb the shipping costs and what carrier will be used? Use the key words to answer questions regarding your distribution plan. Back up your decisions with statistical reports, rate sheets from shippers, contracts with manufacturer's representatives or any other supporting documents. If you are involved in a service business, will you provide in-shop service? Will you make service calls, and, if so, how will mileage costs be handled? What is your planned response time to fill your customers' needs?

List the pros and cons of the various methods of distribution and give reasons for your choices. Present alternatives. For example, if United Parcel Service, your major shipper, were to go on strike, how would you distribute your products? If your mobile service van were to break down, do you have a vehicle which could be used as backup? Provide for a smooth business flow.

Advertising

Advertising presents the message to your customer that your product or service is good and desirable. Tailor your advertising to your target market. Your marketing research will have spelled out which television and radio stations and which publications are of interest to your target market. Those are the ones you will use. Analyze your competitors' advertising in these publications. Be ready to back up your decisions. Include copies of your promotional materials, such as brochures, direct mail advertisements and flyers. Tell the lender where you will put your advertising dollars, why you chose those methods, how your message will reach your target market, when your advertising campaign will begin, how much your plan will cost and what format your advertising will take.

Pricing

Your pricing structure is critical to the success of your business and is determined through market research and analysis of financial considerations. Basic marketing strategy is to price within the range between the price ceiling and the price floor. The price ceiling is determined by the market; it is the highest cost a consumer will pay for a product or service and is based on perceived value.

What is the competition charging? What is the quality of the product or service you are offering? What is the nature of the demand and what is the image you are projecting? The price floor is the lowest amount at which you can offer a product or service, meet all your costs and still make your desired profit. Consider all costs -- raw materials, office overhead, shipping, vehicle expense, taxes, loan and interest payments and owner draws are a few. The profitable business operates between the price ceiling and the price floor. The difference allows for discounts, bad debt and returns. Be specific about how you arrived at your pricing structure and leave room for some flexibility.

Positioning --- predetermining the perceived value in the eyes of the consumer --- can be accomplished through promotional activities. To be successful, you must decide what your product or service offers that your competitor's does not and promote it as the uni☐ue benefit. Very few items on the market have universal appeal your product or service cannot be all things to all people. However, if you position your product or service properly, prospective purchasers or users will immediately recognize its benefits to them.

CHAPTER SEVEN

SWOT (So-What) Analysis

One thing that makes my palms sweat when reviewing a business plan or strategy document is a SWOT analysis. Reading one of those two-by-two tables makes me think that my generally very smart, commercial, rational clients, have decided to illustrate what they learned at primary school, or have accidentally inserted a no-idea-is-stupid whiteboard printout from the start of a brainstorming session.

I'm not saying that SWOT doesn't have its place at the beginning of the strategy development process; it does, especially if you start with the "O".

O, for opportunity, forces you to take a moment to look around and speculate where the future pools of profit might be, which is especially useful for bringing out those areas that you're currently not doing anything about.

S(trengths) helps you realise where your sources of competitive advantage might lie.

W(eaknesses) forces you to be realistic about what may need improving, and traits that might put you at a disadvantage.

T(hreats) forces you to look at those things coming over the horizon that might sink you below the water line.

This forced lookaround for factors that may be important is, in my experience, the entire benefit of SWOT. But it's only of value if you go on to test properly which ones are true and material. Unfortunately, most plans that I see stop with the SWOT output, and bung the list unqualified into the document. This is worse than useless; it's foolhardy, because it can set in train a series of actions that are based on barely-substantiated speculation.

From the long list of strengths, weaknesses, opportunities and threats that emerge in the SWOT analysis, how do you know which are actually true as opposed to speculation? Which are material and will affect the entire future of your business, and which are pretty much irrelevant? Which ones should you deliberately not do something about, for example the weakness in high-end products that would kill your cost advantage if you addressed it? How do you know which opportunities are the ones to put time and money into, and which are the ones to deprioritise?

If you recognise SWOT's limitations, and treat it as a start point, from which you do some testing with facts, then you can create something valuable from this motley list of brainstormed hypotheses.

Start with the opportunities and ask some standard commercial ☐uestions. How big are they? How well positioned are we to exploit them versus everyone else? How much does it cost to start exploiting each of them? How sustainable is the profit stream that comes from each? Which of them is the most valuable use of a dollar of investment or an hour of management time? If the business case of any one of them stacks up, what do we do next to get there?

Do the same kind of reality check and so-what test with the strengths, weaknesses and threats. And you will end up with a short list of credible opportunities and actions, which I promise will pay back the additional time a hundred-fold.

CHAPTER EIGHT

Tips on preparing a professional business plan

Investors are interested in the finished plan, not the process you went through to produce it. They prefer to see a well-prepared document from which they can gain a good sense of the risks and opportunities involved on the first read-through. When preparing your plan, the themes of customer value and potential return should run through the descriptions of your business objectives.

The three phases of the Competition provide a general structure for preparing your plan. The three phases build upon one another such that the contribution for a previous phase will become a major portion of the following phase, supplemented with additional elements.

How you carry out the work within each phase is up to you. The following tips are designed to help you.

Plan your approach

Drawing up a business plan is a very complex undertaking. Many variables must be considered and analyzed systematically, in a logical order. A detailed outline should be made as soon as the first ideas are laid down. It is smart to do your planning along the lines of a business plan, or according to your business system (e.g. R&D, production, marketing, sales, delivery and administration).

You should also number your topics and note any references. Using a word processing program with a spreadsheet is helpful. All reference material should be sorted by topic. Do the same with notes from discussions.

Tailor key ☐uestions to your specific project

Using a set of ☐uestions is helpful in preparing your business plan. Which ☐uestions should be asked and which answers included in the plan is determined by the type of value created, the product, service, or degree of technological sophistication, and what the readers need to know.

In other words, you are not re☐uired to answer each ☐uestion, nor must you answer all questions in e☐ual depth. It is up to you to decide which ☐uestions are relevant to your undertaking and necessary to understand it. You must also consider whether there are other ☐uestions to be answered beyond those that have already been provided.

Focus on the final poduct

In projects of this kind, there is always a danger of getting lost in the details of each analysis. Step back from time to time and ask yourself whether the data provided is not already sufficient and whether further analysis will really be beneficial.

I also recommend that you limit the length of the results for each of the three Competition phases. You will save a lot of time and energy if you stick to the recommended lengths from the beginning of your planning.

Seek support early

Gathering support from many different parties will be important in this Competition. Teaming up early is one such form of support. Teams with complementary technical and entrepreneurial experience can delegate assignments according to the talents of the individual team members. This will help ensure that the work will be performed efficiently.

Do not hesitate to seek help from outside sources as soon as you need it. Contact experts and experienced entrepreneurs whom you meet at the get-togethers.

Keep testing your plan

A winning entry will be easy to understand and follow. Therefore, it is important to present your idea to a test audience along the way. People outside the competition who criti☐ue your plan before you submit it can identify weaknesses and even give your work fresh impetus.

CHAPTER NINE

Risk, Return and Exit

Sooner rather than later the prospective investor will ask himself: What is the risk, what sort of return can I expect for bearing this risk and how can I realise my investment, i.e. exit? There are two ways of tackling the first issue, that of risk. Either, address the risks associated with the proposal at each stage at which these occur, e.g. productions, sales, staffing etc... or, alternatively, conclude your plan with a separate section devoted specifically to risk and the related issues of return and exit.

Whichever option you choose it is important that you are: realistic in appraising risks; neither selective nor over pessimistic about the difficulties; clear about how you intend minimising the risks; aware of potential objections to your proposals.

Bear in mind that the investor's objective is to maximise the investment gain, not exercise control over the business. What he needs to know is how valuable your company might become (and therefore what is the expected future value of the initial investment), and what routes are open to realising a capital gain.

CHAPTER TEN

Financial planning

Financial planning assists you in evaluating whether your business concept will be profitable and can be financed. To this end, the results of all preceding chapters must be compiled and consolidated. Projected growth in value results from the planned cash flows from your operative business. These are revealed through li☐uidity planning, which also provides information on your various financing needs. In addition, the profit situation of your business can be seen in the income statement. This statement is also necessary according to commercial and tax law. There are many ways to present the figures.

Planned income statement. Whether a company's assets grow or diminish depends on the bottom line at the end of a year. The income statement can help you forecast this.

In contrast to liquidity planning (= planned cash flow), an income statement focuses on the issue of whether transactions lead to an increase (= revenue) or a decrease (= expense) in the net worth of your business (defined as the sum of all assets minus debt).

Go through your entire business plan and decide whether your assumptions will lead to revenues or expenses and, if so, how high they will be. If you are in doubt about the exact amount of costs your business will incur, gather ☐uotes and estimates. Do not forget to cover the cost of your personal living expenses. In the case of a limited liability company, this would be the salary of your general manager.

List write offs in your investment and depreciation planning. The cost of investments themselves, i.e., the purchase price of the investment, is not included in the income statement because the amount paid out does not lead to a change in the net worth of the business.

Material costs comprise all expenses for raw materials, auxiliaries, expendable supplies and purchased goods and services. Your planned human resource expenditure includes wages and salaries plus social security contributions and taxes and is listed under personnel costs.

For the purpose of simplification, the category "other costs" is treated as a collective item, including among other things, rent, insurance, office supplies, postage, advertising and legal counsel.

Finally, calculate the difference between all revenue and expenses in a financial year, by which you will arrive at a net profit or net loss for the year. This will give you an overview of the operating result, but it will not give you a reliable assessment of your level of li□uid funds. For this, you will need li□uidity planning.

Sales of your product or service may be booked in the current financial year, even though payment does not occur until the next; you will need to list the sales revenue even though the money has not yet been deposited into your accounts. The same is true for expenses.

The income statement is generally planned in annual intervals. To enhance the accuracy of your planning for the first year, you should make monthly forecasts. For the second year, □uarterly, and for the third, fourth, and fifth year, continue to make annual projections.

Li□uidity planning

Your company must have a certain amount of cash on hand at any given time in order to avoid becoming insolvent, which leads to bankruptcy that will mean the financial ruin of your business. Detailed li□uidity planning should help ensure a positive cash flow. The principle is simple: Receipts are compared directly to disbursements. Please note that writing or receiving an invoice does not mean that the money is already in your account or that you have paid the bill.

Liquidity planning is concerned with the actual date of payment when the money actually comes in or goes out. Thus, li□uidity planning involves only those transactions which cause a change in your cash reserves. Depreciation, liabilities, and non-market output are not included.

Lay out the amount and timing of all the payments you expect. Your company is solvent when the sum of its receipts is greater than the sum of its disbursements at any given time. You will have to draw on capital for those times when this planning does not cover all expenses. The sum of all these individual payments will e□ual the total capital re□uired for that planning interval.

The farther you look into the future, the more uncertain your planning will be. Li□uidity planning should thus be carried out every month for the first year, □uarterly for the second year and only annually for the third, fourth and fifth years.

Projected balance sheet

Venture capitalists are interested in seeing how your assets are expected to grow. This is presented in the shape of a projected balance sheet. Here, the type and value of the assets are placed on the asset side of the balance sheet across from the source of the capital on the liabilities side. As with the income statement, there is a standard accounting format, re□uired by law, for balance sheets. They are prepared at annual intervals.

Financing needs

Li□uidity planning enables you to determine the amount of capital you will need and when you will need it, but it does not indicate how these needs will be met. I basically distinguish between equity (investors have a stake in the business) versus loan capital, which is borrowed from outside sources.

"You can't get something for nothing," the saying goes; the same is true of money. Your family may ask little in return for financial assistance, professional lenders are more demanding. All the management team can offer investors for their cash is a promise – not exactly a good position from which to negotiate. Nevertheless, you have a good chance of being financially successful if business goes well, because professional investors also have an interest in top performance from the team. Be clear about your needs and expectations and those of your investors.

If you are seeking a long-term commitment and are satisfied with a small company, you are probably well advised to make use of family funds and loans from friends and banks.

You will retain a majority shareholding, but you are significantly restricting your chances for growth.

If, however, you desire rapid expansion, you will want to procure venture capital. Venture capitalists will generally expect to obtain a large share of the company, you may in fact have to relin□uish the majority of the e□uity. Professional investors, however, are not interested in managing the business as long as you meet your targets, even if they have the majority shareholding. They have, after all, invested in the management team in order to lead it to success. They will support you actively with their management skills and contribute specialty knowledge such as legal or marketing expertise, ties, and contacts.

A deal can be very complicated. It is always advisable to contact experienced entrepreneurs and get the expert advice of trustees, tax advisors and lawyers. You may also want to gather a number of bids from various investors.

CHAPTER ELEVEN

Summary

Your business plan is, first and foremost, a sales tool. It is essential that it looks good and reads well. Professional presentation is critical.

Beyond this you should observe the following guidelines:

1. The text should be cogent, concise and clearly laid out.

2. Focus on key issues, avoid extraneous details. Knowing what to leave out is just as important as knowing what to include.

3. State clearly what makes your product different or better and exactly where you intend focussing. Trying to do too much is indicative of a poor understanding of what you could do best.

4. Formulate objectives that are unambiguous, consistent, credible and compatible with industry experience.

5. Show that you really understand how your target market operates, what your customers want, how you will distinctively meet these needs and on what basis you will compete successfully.

6. Display a clear understanding of your investor's needs and interests.

7. Avoid complete infatuation with your product and how it will be produced.

8. Demonstrate that the team you have assembled has the balance and the track record to exploit the market opportunity as well as the determination to stick with the venture.

9. Openly address risks and problems, explaining how you intend dealing with them.

10. Ensure that the plan is intelligible and complete in itself, having no need of additional data or explanation. Think also about how you could most compellingly sell your plan in a ten minute oral presentation.

Following these tips and the information in this book, and you should be able to draft the business plan you need to move forward with your business.

***

Enjoy this book? Here's some other Martell Books titles you may be interested in.

'The Lean Channel: YouTube for Entrepreneurs'

'Have you ever wanted to start a business centered around producing YouTube videos? Having trouble convincing viewers to become subscribers? This book serves as a guide for the complete novice instructing in how to get started on your path to becoming a new media sensation and make money.'

http://martellbooks.com/2015/11/30/the-lean-channel-youtube-for-entrepreneurs/

'Agile SCRUM for Film-makers: How to Produce Movies & TV Shows In Half the Time'

If you want to use SCRUM to develop movies and TV shows, 'Agile SCRUM for Film-makers' is the reference guide you've been looking for. Author Carey Martell explains the principles and method of SCRUM, and describes flexible, proven approaches that can help you implement it far more effectively in your production team.

http://martellbooks.com/2015/11/30/agile-scrum-for-film-makers-how-to-produce-movies-tv-shows-in-half-the-time/

'Facebook Marketing: Guide to Strategies That Don't Suck'

In this workbook you will get a crash-course guide in how to setup a branded Facebook Page for your business and grow an audience using both organic (free) strategies. You will also learn how to conduct paid ad campaigns using promoted posts and Facebook Power Editor.

http://martellbooks.com/2015/12/23/facebook-marketing-guide-strategies-dont-suck/

'YouTube Sponsorships: How Creators Like You Can Fund Your Channel'

Each year companies spend $17 Billion on sponsorships. This is an ideal source of funding to tap into for any YouTube creators. However, many video bloggers simply have no idea what a good sponsorship deal is. They do videos for either low or no money that, if they were more knowledgeable, would have earned them six figure deals. Sport athletes and film actors don't do endorsements for free. Why should you?

http://martellbooks.com/2015/11/30/youtube-sponsorships-how-creators-like-you-can-fund-your-channel-2/

www.ingramcontent.com/pod-product-compliance
Lightning Source LLC
Chambersburg PA
CBHW070430190526
45169CB00003B/1483